HOW TO TALK TO ANYONE

IMPROVE SOCIAL SKILLS, GAIN SELF-
CONFIDENCE, AND BOOST YOUR CHARISMA TO
INSTANTLY CONNECT WITH ANYONE

STEVEN HOPKINS

INTRODUCTION

All around us are people with independent thoughts and feelings, family members that love them, and pasts that made them who they are. All of these people have different feelings, thoughts, opinions, and traumas that might differ from your own, or maybe they're the same as the things you feel. Though most of us all know this, other people can still be so terrifying to talk to!

Maybe you've tried different methods of talking to people that have never helped. Perhaps you took an acting class, went to a speed dating session, or even talked to a professional about how to talk to other people. If after you've tried all this, and you still feel like you can't talk to people, you think, "So, there's no other way"? Well, actually, there is. All it involves is looking within yourself to determine what you need in order to learn how to talk to anyone.

How I Transformed My Life

I was once a person crippled with social anxiety, but now, I'm happily married with two kids, and am a personal trainer, an entrepreneur, a life and motivation coach. What changed me? Well, one of the things that started my transformation was improving my small talk. Yes, sure, there were other factors that helped me, but these were linked to my self-confidence. My low self-confidence meant that I found it difficult to speak up and connect with others. Linda Vale, the woman who would eventually become my life coach, helped me to see that the separation of my parents, when I was six, had had a major impact on my life. I had fallen into a pattern of hiding myself away from others and as I grew into an adult my lifestyle choices meant that I wasn't in as great a shape as I could have been. I had become reliant upon frozen meals for dinner and got very little exercise. Certainly this was a reflection of how little I thought of myself.

My chance encounter with Linda, on the train home one night, made me look at my life in a different light. If you read my book: Self-Discipline to Exercise, then I'm sure you know my story. For years, I tried different practices, bought into certain "programs," and even took medication to improve my social anxiety. What I found works the most, however, is starting small. I've accepted the fact that there is no small fix. There's no pill that's going to make me the most intelligent person in the world that always has the best conversations, constantly making meaningful connections. I can't just turn a switch and change my personality.

I can, however, look inwards to determine what needs to be done to make me a more confident, happy, and healthy person. I understand now that talking to people is a practice, and some days are going to be harder than others. With the right methods, techniques, and practices, however, I know that I have the ability to talk to anyone. It's a freeing feeling and one that's like lifting a weight off my shoulders. I'm going to share my secrets with you now so that you, too, can have the ability to talk to anyone.

It can be hard to grow yourself. You might have to confront certain issues or recognize unhealthy behavior in order to improve certain aspects of your life. Some days, I just wanted to give up and lie in bed instead of head to a meeting where I knew I would have to do a lot of talking.

There was a time in my life when I was looking for a job, and I had a couple of interviews coming up. I would get so nervous before the interaction that I would feel sick to my stomach. I canceled an interview with someone, expecting that I just wouldn't get that job. The fear of the interview felt awful, and the negative feelings didn't disappear once I canceled the interview. They just manifested in other ways.

The person I was supposed to have the interview with reached out to me and ended up giving me a second chance. I went to the interview and nailed it, landing the job. The fear the first time around was bad, but the feeling of getting the job was great. I realized at that moment that confronting my fears was hard, but it was so much harder to continually live in a state of fear. Instead of being scared all the time, I now am only scared in certain situations. And when that fear creeps up, I have the tools needed to silence all the negative thoughts that might make me want to run and hide.

The Importance of Small Talk

The first and most important step on the road in learning to talk to anyone involves small talk. This is just the practice of general discussion with a person on the surface. Small talk can sometimes feel as though it's unimportant, but in reality, it helps to create the stepping stones that will lead to a greater connection.

Small talk is also an important practice in growing confidence. Even if you will never see that person at the coffee shop again, it can still be an important part in developing crucial social skills that you need in other areas.

Is This Book for You?

There's a reason you're reading this book. Maybe you've noticed work relationships lacking because you can't speak up and be confident with other people. Perhaps you're tired of being so afraid to leave your house because of the social interactions you might have to endure. No matter what you might be feeling, remember that you should be proud for recognizing that your social skills can improve. This book is for you, and it's going to help you achieve everything that you've wanted for yourself. If you can learn to talk to anyone, you can start to get what you want from others, create more meaningful connections, and improve your life altogether.

1. CONQUERING YOUR SMALL TALK FEAR

> *Courage is resistance to fear, mastery of fear, not absence of fear.*
>
> — MARK TWAIN

THE THING we have to remember about conquering our fears is that the anxiety and worry won't go away, it just becomes easier to manage. For example, if you're afraid of flying but you have to travel for work, every time you get on the plane, you're still going to get scared, but by the 20th flight, you're a lot less worried than you were the first time around.

The way to learn to manage this fear is through practice. Start small by having conversations with people that you know well and trust. Be actively listening to them and yourself to make sure that you can pick up on what works and what might not through each conversation.

Change Your Limiting Beliefs

We often limit what we believe ourselves capable of. We do this by limiting our imaginations, or denying that we are capable of more than what we see before us. This is something that I did again and again before meeting Linda, my life coach, and beginning my journey of transformation. I refused to see myself as anything other than an overweight guy sitting behind a desk all day and eating frozen pizzas for dinner. If you've read my book on how to build Self-Discipline to Diet, then you know what I went through to finally change that limiting belief and my identity.

Changing your limiting beliefs can be a first important step in overcoming your small talk fear. When you're overly invested in your own version of truth, you can really block a lot of people around you. To make sure that you're maintaining an open mind towards new conversations, you have to identify your own perspective and the boundaries that it might create.

Sometimes, we become so sure of our own realities because it's the most reliant thing we have. The world is so full of chaos and mystery that it's important to make sure that we have a solid set of beliefs and morals to give us at least somewhat of a limit on the things we do and think. Sometimes, however, this can be limiting rather than encouraging.

Embrace a Growth Mindset

To change your limiting beliefs, you have to embrace a growth mindset around conversations in general, including small talk. Stop looking at conversations as methods to get what you want. Don't avoid small talk with someone just because you don't think it will bring you any value. Every person has a different perspective so it's important to know people on an individual level, not a transactional one.

The best way to encourage your brain to continue growing is by reminding yourself that there really isn't a stopping point. There's no limit on all the valuable things that you know, so the more you open yourself to different experiences, the more you gain from each and every moment. Every experience, conversation, and moment we have, whether it's good or bad, is valuable.

Even moments we sit in a waiting room for hours can add value, as long as we look for the importance in that experience. You might have a conversation in which you learn something, or you could help make someone else's day even better.

How to Stop Being Self Conscious

If only we had the confidence that we believe others have. The truth is, even the most confident, brave, and courageous people have moments of fear. Even the most famous pop star that belts her heart out on stage week after week might continually have anxiety or dread over the concerts, fearful of what could happen. Hard to believe, right?

Sometimes, you just have to let the act of confidence come before you feel it. There are going to be moments when you just want to run back to bed and hide under the covers, but you just have to put on your shoes, take a breath, put on a smile and face whatever challenges you have.

There's no quick pill you can take that's going to make you stop being self-conscious. Instead, you have to learn different methods that you can implement each time you feel like you might be having a self-conscious moment. Here are some tips that can help you get started:

1. Don't put people on a pedestal. At the end of the day, we're all individuals with good and bad moments, thoughts we wish we didn't have, and regrets we like to keep secret.
2. Don't say anything to yourself you wouldn't say to your best friend. You wouldn't tell your best friend that what they have to say is stupid, so why do you allow your mind to say that to yourself?
3. Cut out negative thoughts. Those thoughts have no value unless you give it to them.
4. Remind yourself that most people are just as self-conscious, if not more, than you. They're more likely to focus on their own issues rather than any small thing you might have said that you believe to be embarrassing.

Small Talks Are Not Stupid

Sometimes, Small talk can feel meaningless, especially if you don't go beyond the current weather or what you might've eaten for breakfast. However, you have to remember that small talks are just the first step towards getting to bigger conversations.

Think of a relationship you might have with a small child or animal. You wouldn't walk up to them right away and just pick them up, hug and kiss them, right? It's tempting depending on their level of cuteness, but you would first probably crouch to their level, stick out a hand, and let them get to know you first. Think of small talk as this moment of letting them "sniff your hand."

Small talk serves a purpose for meaningful relationships. You might have met your friend in the strangest way without any small talk, but not all relationships will form in this way. Small talk is your chance to get a sense of what a person is like. Are they nervous, shy, or confident? Do they have a good sense of humor or do you need to be careful to not offend them with your jokes?

Practice Makes Perfect

The best way to practice having good conversation is to do them! If you have to, start online. Sometimes just getting involved in forums allows you to start practicing putting your thoughts into words.

From there, go outside and have conversations with

strangers. It's the opposite of what our parents told us to do, but don't be afraid to start a conversation with the person in line at the coffee shop, or someone sitting next to you on the train. A lot of people don't want to be talked to, so if you pick up on the idea that they don't want a conversation, simply move onto another person. Don't force someone else to talk if they don't want to, so find people that actually want to have a conversation to practice with.

These methods of practice are easier because you know that if you do embarrass yourself, you might never see them again. Stop thinking and start doing, it's the only way for improvement to actually happen.

What we've learned

- Fear can sometimes be a manifestation of other fear. If you remind yourself to expand your mind and no longer have limiting beliefs, you can also overcome your fear of talking to other people.
- Your small talk fear comes from a place of being self-conscious. Overcoming your lack of confidence will make small talk so much easier.

- There isn't anything stupid about small talk. It is the way to get to more important conversations that will lead to stronger connections and relationships.

Making a good impression is crucial, and we'll go over that in the next chapter to ensure you leave a lasting imprint.

2. SEVEN SECONDS TO MAKE A GOOD FIRST IMPRESSION

> *Whatever makes an impression on the heart seems lovely in the eye.*
>
> — SAADI

YES. You heard the title of the chapter correctly. It only takes seven seconds for you to make a good first impression. It might be in the form of a smile, or maybe in how you shake their hand. The first thing you say to someone could be important, or maybe they don't even hear what you had to say and instead just know they like you based on the warm tones of your soothing voice. There are many different ways to make an impression, but at the end of the day, the most important thing is making sure it's a good impression.

To do so, you have to first pay attention to your body language. You may or may not know this already, but your body language will tell the other person a lot about you. We don't all have to be body language experts to have the knowledge to tell if someone is uncomfortable or not. People who roll their eyes or avoid eye contact might be bored, or they could just be really tired. There are plenty of indications we can take from someone else in any given conversation, so we have to remember that other people have the same methods of understanding us as well.

This is something that I came to truly understand when I was making pitches for funding for different business projects that I was setting up. I could tell from observing body language, whether somebody was genuinely interested in funding me, or whether they were just being polite. It was during a pitch for one of my failed businesses, the line of gym wear, that I realized I had developed a sixth sense when it came to body language. It was also at this point that I realized the importance of my own body language.

The Importance of Making a Good First Impression

How many people did you meet once and form an opinion about? Sometimes, a first impression is all it takes for us to form the idea that we aren't interested in a certain person. While you can control whether or not you allow a first impression to define another person, you can't control whether or not someone is going to base their idea of you from a first impression. To make sure you're eliminating the chance of someone else disliking you after the first time you meet, you have to focus on making good small talk. In my book: How to Make People Like You, I go more in depth into the techniques and body language to make a good first impression, but for now, all you have to understand is how important it is.

The key to a successful small talk is a good first impression, and vice versa. You can't have one without the other. It can cause anxiety knowing that you could alter someone's perception of you within seconds, but that's why you need to make sure you practice different conversations to find what works for you.

First impressions have a significant effect on the future of a relationship. Whether we like it or not, people will form opinions of us right away. These impressions might eventually get proved wrong, or maybe it's just the way they see us forever.

When meeting people for the first time, you should strive to give them an impression of being friendly as well as approachable. There's nothing wrong with being too nice to someone the first time you meet them. Being "too nice," only becomes an issue later when people let others take advantage of them. Now, let me talk to you about some easy tricks you can use to make others like you instantly.

Dress the way You Want to be Addressed

Always dress respectably. The better dressed you are, the better impression you'll make. This doesn't necessarily mean wearing designer suits or dresses, but rather, putting effort into showing that you care about what you're wearing. When you give people the idea that you want to dress respectably and that you are trying to make a good first impression, it'll show.

Making an Impression with Your Clothes

Picking out what to wear is always specific to what the event is that you might be attending. Is it brunch with a college? An international conference? Maybe a first date with the lady or gentleman you met in a party? You have to gauge a situation before going to make sure you show up appropriately dressed.

Expressing Yourself with Your Clothes

To make people remember you, you can make an effort and express yourself with what you are wearing. However, be careful when you are attending some professional events. If you only like wearing tie dye, bedazzled, and ripped up clothing, that's great! But make sure you stick to something professional when the time calls for it. If you identify yourself with your clothes too much, people might make assumptions too fast about your personality and character.

Having an Open Body Language

If you're not careful with what body language you have, you could be sending the wrong message. It's crucial to become more aware of your body so that you can better evaluate how you might be giving off symbols in certain situations.

Stand straight. Not too stiff to where you look like a royal guard, but enough to where people can tell you actually care about being there.

Keep your hands visible. If people can see your hands, they'll be much more likely to trust you.

Have your shoulders relaxed. Tense shoulders create

tense situations and can cause you unnecessary stress. Whenever you're talking to someone or even just when you're alone, check to make sure your shoulders are relaxed. Many of us don't even realize how much tension we're holding.

Share Your Smile With the World

When meeting someone new, a bright, genuine, and warm smile will always make things easier. Your smile is the greatest social tool you've ever been given. There are so many different situations that can be improved just with a smile.

A warm smile goes a long way toward making the right first impression. It shows you're friendly, likely happy, and welcoming to the new person.

A smile is a friend maker. You have the ability to make friends with anyone just by spreading a big smile across your face.

Eye Contact

Eye contact is always important when meeting a new person. If your eyes are shifty, people will start to wonder if they can trust you. If you can't maintain eye contact and instead are rolling your eyes or looking around the room, it makes the other person wonder if you actually care about being there and talking to them.

You don't want to stare directly into their eyes for too long, as it might make them feel uncomfortable, but you should do your best to try and maintain eye contact.

Handshakes

In any professional settings, understanding the art of a proper handshake is essential to making a good first impression. Your handshakes should always be firm. This might be the first impression anyone will have of you, so if you're too hesitant to shake their hand, or you let your arm hang loose, it might give them the wrong impression. You can really impress others with a firm handshake, but don't go overboard and try so hard that you break their hand.

Voice and Tone

Speak firmly. How you talk to others is the most important part of a conversation. Some people are soft-spoken and that's fine. However, be sure to keep a firm diction so that others can understand what you're saying.

Make sure you're loud enough to show confidence as well. If you're too quiet and people consistently can't hear what you're saying, eventually, they'll stop listening altogether.

Imagine one of several powerful people you know, do they seem confident when they speak? Do they speak firmly, with a high volume? If you can picture a person that fits this confident image, try to imitate this person when you speak. Observe the tone and voice when he or she speaks. Practice speaking with your partner, your family or a friend you trust. Believe me, you will start to speak confidently in no time.

What we've learned

- Your body language plays a huge part in the lasting impression you'll have on another person.
- Be aware of your clothing choices, how much you smile, what your voice and tone are like, and how much eye contact you make to make sure the other person is remaining engaged.
- Your first impression can define what the future relationship might look like, so it's

important to make sure that you're doing your best to start off on the right track.

What's next? What should I say after that handshake, smile and eye contact? Well, don't worry. We are getting there! You will learn how to properly introduce yourself and make others remember you in the next chapter.

3. HOW TO INTRODUCE YOURSELF

> *Everyone you will ever meet knows something you don't.*
>
> — Bill Nye

Making an impression upon someone is often down to how well you introduce yourself. Let's face it, we'll never get another opportunity to make a first impression on someone. It's important to remember that while it can be helpful to develop a consistent way to regularly introduce yourself to new contacts, it won't work very well if it doesn't feel natural. The way I met my wife, Michelle, for example. Michelle met me at the gym where I was working as a personal trainer. She was looking for some hints and tips on gaining muscle tone, and I was happy to help. It was a natural setting, a natural meeting. There were no airs, or affectations and that is what this chapter is all about: introducing yourself in the most natural, but effective, way possible.

Greet Appropriately

A greeting is the very first step when a conversation starts. Even if you've seen someone around, it's always important to make sure that you have a formal introduction with this person. Shake their hand, look them in the eye and learn their name.

Like we mentioned earlier, smile is a powerful tool to make people like you. Greet a person with a friendly smile, and you are on your way to building a good new relationship.

Always follow the other person's lead when greeting as well. You want to make sure that you're not too overbearing in the beginning to where they feel uncomfortable, or so shy and timid that they don't remember you.

Make sure to first start by asking them how they're doing. Most people will say "good" or "fine," but it's not the words that matter. It's how they say these things. A rushed tone might mean they don't have time to chat. They'll probably say good even if they're feeling really down. You can base what you do next from how their voices sounded in the beginning.

Determining the Level of Formality

The formality of a situation is important in order to determine the appropriate greeting. Sometimes, you have to make sure to shake their hand and give a full introduction of your name and title. Other times might only call for a simple, "Hey what's up, I'm Steven."

In order to determine the level of formality, make a judgment of the situation. Are the people you're meeting important in maintaining your status? Maybe they're a client for your business, one of your bosses, or even your girlfriend's parents. If these people have deciding power over you in any way, you should give them a formal introduction. This doesn't always mean handing a business card over with a firm handshake. You just have to be appropriate and make sure that you're not coming off in any way that would suggest you don't care.

You can be too formal sometimes as well, which makes

others feel as though you're a robot or unapproachable. To make sure you're not being too formal, always offer a smile and be certain to ask about them. Ask how their day has been, how their flight coming in was, or if they need something like a glass of water. Make sure that the other person understands that you care about meeting them while also assuring them you're an approachable person.

Introduce Yourself Properly

Introducing yourself goes beyond saying your name. Sometimes, if it's a situation in which you're meeting for the first time and they have no idea who you are, you might want to include a title, such as producer, business manager, or something else that allows the other person to associate you with a position. You wouldn't have to do this if you're meeting other friends or people that aren't affected by your job title, but in a business setting, it's good to make sure there's no confusion about who you are or what your purpose might be.

Your introduction should tell people who you are, and it should encourage people to engage with you. After the initial moment of sharing names, it's important to have a light conversation about who you are as well. You should first ask how they're doing, and when they ask you, always tell them that you're doing "good," "great," or "fine." I know some of you might think this is inauthentic, but when you think about how important the first impression is, I think you will agree with me on this point. After all, we can always turn to the people we already built a relationship with to express our true feelings. So, even if you're in a bad mood, you don't want to tell them you're doing "bad" right away, or else they might get the impression that you're a grumpy person, or someone who often complains. Instead, you could just say something like, "I'm great! I had a long flight but I'm very excited to be here."

Introduce yourself in a memorable way, and one in which people will like and appreciate you. You don't want to do all the talking in an introduction as you want the other person to get the chance to talk about themselves. You do, however, want to still make sure you're a part of the conversation as this might be the only chance you get to talk to someone. Don't talk over anyone, but make sure that the other person at least gets an idea or two about who you are and what makes you an individual.

Give Them a Chance to Introduce Themselves

The introduction is not complete without other people introducing themselves. Especially in a business setting, you might want to just start talking right away about work, so you can get things rolling. You have to be patient, however, and instead wait for them to lead the conversation. They might have just done a lot of traveling themselves, so maybe they just want to get a drink at the hotel bar and have a chat for a bit.

Even in an interview setting, you might feel the urge to start talking about yourself and your qualities, but still ask how the other person is doing and give them a chance to start talking about themselves and their day. This helps make you look like an understanding person with good listening skills, whilst also giving both of you the chance to make a deeper connection before going any further with your relationship.

What we've learned

- An introduction is the foundation for how a relationship is going to be built. You have to make sure that you're properly introducing yourself, so the other person gets an idea of who you are.

- Make sure the other person has the chance to introduce themselves as well. You don't want to talk about yourself too much and not give them a chance to speak at all.
- Make sure you're judging the level of formality correctly. You don't want to make anyone feel uncomfortable.

You've learned how to introduce yourself, and now it's time to find some cool topics to talk about! You will find some great ideas of how to break the ice when starting a conversation. Head over to the next chapter to find out!

4. GREAT CONVERSATION STARTERS TO BREAK THE ICE

> *My idea of good company is the company of clever, well-informed people who have a great deal of conversation; that is what I call good company.*
>
> — JANE AUSTEN

A good conversation starter can transform an awkward, stilted conversation into an interesting, enjoyable discussion. After all, who wants to talk to a boring person? When meeting someone for the first time, you might feel uncomfortable and afraid to speak. But hey, they might be just as nervous as you do!

So when this happens, we need someone to break the ice, and it helps to have a few ideas of good conversation starters.

This chapter includes nine different topics that would be good conversation starters. Within each topic, there are three different questions you can use depending on how close you are with a person. The first one is something you might discuss with someone you don't know very well, and the third is a good starter for someone you have more of a rapport with.

Chat with Them About Their Lifestyle

What plans do you have for the weekend? You could discuss your own plans, and also get to know them a little better based on their activities. If they say, "nothing," then you could start a conversation about how much you enjoy having weekends off, or maybe suggest a movie or show you like that they could watch during their downtime.

Do you have any pets? People love talking about their pets, so you can never go wrong with this topic.

What's something strange about you I could never guess

just from looking? People love talking about themselves, especially sharing small secrets that might ignite the curiosity of the other person.

Ask About Their Traveling

Michelle and I have done so much travelling and I just love it whenever anybody asks us about where we have gone because it gives us the opportunity to relive some great memories and tell some fascinating stories. People are always surprised when we say that we spent a year living in Singapore, setting up a consultancy there. Sure, not everyone will have a story like that, but everyone likes to talk about where they've been.

Do you like flying? There's so much to talk about when it comes to airports, planes, and flying in general. This is something many people relate to, and with this you can also chat with them about your most recent travel experience.

What's the last vacation you went on? Vacations are the greatest things in life, so people are going to love talking about the trips they've been on, or where they might be going.

If you could go anywhere, where would you go? This is a

great topic that could lead to endless conversation. With all the places in the world to go, you won't run out of ideas when you start talking about travel.

Technology Conversations are Always Relevant

What kind of phone do you have? There's a lot to be discussed with the little box in our pockets, so you could really carry the conversation far with just this small question.

Do you spend a lot of time online? The internet is filled with an endless amount of information. You can ask them about their online use, or maybe talk about their favorite sites or YouTube videos they keep up with.

What do you think the future holds for technology? The future of technology is a topic that we pretty much never stop talking about. What do you think about a smart home? Is blockchain the new Internet? Is AI a threat to humanity? It's always going to be relevant, and there's a lot you can connect to with another person.

Discuss Their Personal Style

Where did you get that shirt? Asking about someone's shirt, dress, or other piece of clothing, is a great way to get the conversation going. You could discuss how much you like the store they got it from, or maybe talk about other clothing items that are similar.

Do you like dressing up? If you're at a formal event, this is always a great question to ask. Most people will share that they hate wearing suits or tight dresses, so they'll be more than happy to talk about their distaste for dressing up.

What's a current trend that you can't stand? People enjoy talking about the things that they hate, so you could really open up a long conversation with this question.

Ask About Their Past

Where did you go to school? A lot can be learned about a person and where they might have gone to school.

Did you like growing up in your hometown? By getting to know someone's hometown and their opinion on it, you can really get to know a lot about them.

What's your most embarrassing memory? This is a great discussion topic. It can lead to a hilarious conversation that can really bring you and the other person closer.

Talk About the Future

Do you have any exciting things planned this month? Maybe they're getting married or going on a trip. Finding out what they're doing next can lead to a great conversation.

Does anything about the future scare you? The future can be scary, so this open-ended question could be relatable for many.

What's your biggest goal in life? Not only will you get to know a person a lot based on what their goals might be, but you can also lead the conversation to a great place. I, for example, love talking about the future, and that's because I found my passion by using the list of questions I share in my book: How to Find Your Passion. If finding your passion and purpose is something you're interested in, I think the book can provide you with some valuable insights.

Chatting About the Weather Isn't Always Boring

Isn't it a great day out? This is pretty basic but starting a conversation about the weather can lead to many other great topics as long as you can carry it further than just the temperature.

Do you prefer the cold or the heat? Everyone has an opinion about whether they'd rather be hot or cold, so this is a great topic that could lead to a lot of different discussions.

What's your most beautiful memory about snow? The snow can hold a lot of dear memories for people, so there's a good chance the other person has some experiences they can discuss involving snow.

Discuss about Books and Movies

What's the last movie you saw in theaters? This conversation can lead to the discussion of that specific movie, or just movie theaters in general.

Do you have a large collection of physical media? People love talking about their collections, and you can get to know a person really well based on what media they might own.

What's the strangest movie you've ever seen? This could lead to a really funny conversation, and who knows, maybe even a great movie suggestion.

Random or Weird Conversation Starters

If you could switch places with anyone in this room, who would you pick? A random question like this can let people know you're down to have a funny conversation.

If you could be famous for anything, what would you pick? You can get to know a lot about a person based on their various talents or different desires and wishes.

What one item would you take to the moon with you? This kind of question can lead to other funny questions about what you might do on the moon.

What we've learned

- How you start a conversation is going to be crucial in how the rest of your relationship is built.
- Practice different conversation starters so that

you're prepared next time a conversation gets boring.

- Remember to talk about general things, and always ask questions to keep the other person engaged in conversation.

You have learned so much about how to make a good first impression and how to start an interesting conversation. You may not believe there's more to it, but there really is! Head on over to the next chapter where we discuss some important small talk tricks you'd need to understand and practice. You ready? Well, let's keep up the good work and keep learning!

5. WHAT TO SAY – SMALL TALK TOPICS AND TECHNIQUES

 Small talk is the biggest talk we do.

— SUSAN ROANE

SOMETIMES, small talk can feel meaningless. It might involve the weather, or maybe just a small chat about the things that surround us. But think about this, the more you think something is meaningless, the more you are inclined to not do it. And you are here to learn the art of talking to anyone, right? Seriously, you have to get the idea that small talk is meaningless out of your head. Just think of it as a means to an end. If done well, a small talk can lead to bigger and greater things that you wouldn't have gotten to. So, with that said, let's dive right in and see what are other things you need to pay attention when it comes to small talk.

Discussing General Things

Bring up general topics when starting off with small talk. You don't want to get into the most recent political election, or the news about global warming right away. Instead, find something relatable on a human level to get things going. Often, this might just be the weather, the food, or the event you're participating, but that can lead to a greater discussion.

You might start off by saying, "Wow, the lighting in this restaurant is beautiful," which is a simple and general idea. The other person might just say, "Yeah," and then you both sit in silence until your other colleagues show up. Or, you can say something more open-ended, such as, "The lighting is beautiful in here. I would love to have something like this in my house." Then the other person might ask where you live, or you can start talking about the other style aspects of the restaurant you like. You could ask a question too like, "Have you been to this restaurant before?" or if you know they haven't, say something like, "This reminds me of a restaurant back home." All of these kinds of comments or questions could lead to a bigger discussion, even though you simply started off chatting about the place that you're in.

Ask Open-Ended Questions

Sometimes, it's easiest to just ask simple yes/no questions when getting into different discussions with new people. If you have the urge to ask a yes/no question, try to think of a way that you can turn it into one that forces them to give a longer response.

"Do you like sushi?" is answered with yes/no. "What kind of sushi do you like?" forces them to at least give a longer answer, even if it's: "I don't like sushi." This is still a chance for you to come back and ask more questions about their comment.

Talk About Relevant Things

While it can be tempting to just discuss the weather, try to find relevancy to what you're discussing. This will help you get closer to making an actual human connection with them. Instead of saying, "I wonder if the rain's ever going to let up," try asking questions or making more relevant statements, like, "Did you bring an umbrella?" Or "I wish I would've worn better shoes for the occasion!" Don't just say what everyone else is thinking. Instead, try to find relevancy in everything you decide to discuss.

Encourage others to talk

Everyone wants to be heard, so you can't go wrong when it comes to asking someone's opinion. Don't force the conversation towards anything political or religious. These kinds of conversations are personal and can make even those that agree on certain topics upset. If you can't think of something to talk about, just ask a simple question. You'll be surprised at how a seemingly trivial question can often turn into an engrossing conversation. It often worked for me when I was at a loss as to what to say next. Once, after a pitch for my energy drink, I accidentally ended up in the elevator with the guy I had been pitching to ten minutes ago. I didn't want it to seem like I had done this deliberately to keep pitching to him, and I struggled to find something to chat about. Eventually I blurted out that I would be pleased to be getting back to my wife who was expecting to soon give birth to our firstborn. I asked if he had any children. He did and was eager to share some advice with me. We ended up chatting all the way to the car park. No, he didn't invest in the energy drink, but he remembered me when I went in to pitch the gym equipment project I was working on, and he did end up investing in that.

Sometimes, we get caught up talking about ourselves. If you feel as though you've been doing most of the talking, try to turn your next comment into a question that can force them to add more to the conversation. For example, if you've been talking about the new car you just drove to your business meeting, ask the other person instead how they got there. Instead of making a comment about yourself, twist it into a question that can help you learn more about them.

Remember People's Names

When you can remember someone's name, it makes he or she feel more important. No one likes to be forgotten.

Mention their name often. If you forgot someone's name, listen for it in other parts of the conversation. Don't be afraid to ask for their name again and just apologize that you forgot.

A trick to remember someone's name is to make sure you know how to spell and pronounce it. Once someone introduces himself or herself to you, repeat his or her name several times in your mind, and link the name with the face.

People love to be called by their own name. So if you really can't remember someone's name, it's better to just admit you forgot their name and ask again rather than go weeks without remembering what to call them.

Stay Curious

When you aren't curious, the conversation dies easily. Continue asking questions and keep the conversation going so that the other person knows that you're legitimately interested in the things they have to say.

Curiosity makes talking to others meaningful. Learning about other people is important, but what we don't realize is that we can also learn a lot about ourselves from the conversations that we have with those around us.

Listen Actively

Actively listen to them talk and don't interrupt them while they're speaking. A person that interrupts others quickly becomes someone no one wants to have a conversation with. If you do accidentally interrupt someone, make sure that you apologize and give him or her the chance to speak. Then ask questions about what they had to say to make sure they know you're engaged.

The most memorable and popular people in the world are those who give their undivided and entire attention. If you notice someone else in a conversation is interrupting others, make sure that you stand up for those that get cut off, saying things like, "Let's hear what Susan has to say," if you noticed she kept getting interrupted.

Feed Their Ego

Make others feel as though their opinion is important. Sometimes, you might not totally agree with what they have to say. You should still remind them that their perspective is interesting and that their opinions are valid.

Feeding someone else's ego is complimenting them. If

you make sure to build someone up instead of trying to find ways to break them down, they'll feel much better leaving the conversation.

Focus on Them

Don't get caught talking about yourself too much. Talking about ourselves is easy to do since we know our own mind better than anyone else. We still need to make sure that we put the attention on other people, giving them the opportunity to speak.

Avoid interrupting or trying to one-up the last bit of information shared. Don't turn a conversation into a competition. Just give them their chance to speak and listen actively so they know they have your attention.

Knowing the general rules of thumb of small talk is important. But maybe you're still looking for more ideas to make talking to anyone that much easier. Here's a list of questions for inspiration.

36 Small Talk Questions to Make Your Life Easier

1. What's the best-hidden spot around here? (or around your hometown)

2. Do you have a hidden talent not many people know about?

3. Have you ever received a piece of advice that still sticks with you?

4. What surprised you most about your current job?

5. If you could adopt an animal that isn't commonly a pet, what would you choose?

6. What's the greatest gift you've ever received?

7. What's a game that you love playing often?

8. If you weren't doing what you're doing now, what job would you have?

9. What do you remember most about your childhood home?

10. If you had a superpower, what would you be?

11. Do you remember getting away with something you should have gotten in trouble for as a child?

12. What show is your biggest guilty pleasure?

13. Do you prefer working long hours within a few days, or do you prefer spreading the work out?

14. What's a song that you know all the words to?

15. If you could adopt any dog, what breed would you choose?

16. What's a movie that you hated that everyone else has seemed to love?

17. Do you like cooking? What kind of dish do you cook the most?

18. Would you rather go to a zoo, a museum, or a national park?

19. What's your favorite holiday?

20. If you could get paid a high amount no matter what, what job would you choose?

21. What's the strangest thing that you've ever eaten?

22. What's the oldest thing you own?

23. If you could go on a road trip anywhere, what would be your destination spot?

24. Have you ever endured what you believe as a paranormal activity?

25. What's your favorite method of transportation?

26. Have you ever thought of an invention that you later discovered already existed?

27. What's the most insane thing a boss has ever asked of you?

28. What's something you hated as a child that you love eating now?

29. If you could bring any dead celebrity back to life, who would you choose? (don't ask about a

dead person in general in case it brings up real-life past trauma)

30. If you could only listen to one band or musician for the rest of your life, who would you choose?

31. If you had to pick only one season to live through all year round, which would you choose?

32. What's a food that you could eat every day?

33. Do you have any good books or movies to recommend I watch or read next?

34. Who do you follow online most closely? (a celebrity they might follow on Instagram)

35. What's the last thing you regret purchasing?

36. Who would you choose as a partner to go on a reality competition show with?

What we've learned

- Keep conversations general so that you don't have to worry about running out of things to say.

- Keep questions open-ended and avoid anything that can be answered with a simple yes or no. You want to make sure you're maintaining a conversation that won't easily fade out.

- Remember people's names and feed their ego so that they feel important in different conversations. The more emphasis you put on them, the better they'll be, and the easier they'll remember you as well.

Once you start off on the right track by making an important introduction, it's time to get deeper into making a more meaningful connection. The next chapter will discuss exactly how that can be achieved.

6. BIGGER TALKS AND CONNECTING WITH ANYONE

> *Making mental connections is our most crucial learning tool, the essence of human intelligence; to forge links; to go beyond the given; to see patterns, relationships, context.*
>
> — MARILYN FERGUSON

YOU SHOULD STRIVE for a place in which you don't worry what other people think of you and find methods to be comfortable with yourself. That being said, forming meaningful connections is still one of the most important parts of life. Not only do you learn more about yourself from interacting with other people, but you can also help others grow as well through your own individual connections.

By this point, you should understand the importance of small talk and some tools needed to make sure you get off to the right start. It's frustrating that I can't personally be with you in these conversations to make sure the right things are being said, but these tools will help you keep up with convos after starting the initial small talk.

Show Enthusiasm

You should look eager to talk to the person. Who wants to talk to someone who seems uninterested? Trying to talk to someone who doesn't have any interest in being there can be very challenging. Instead of thinking about good conversations and what they could add, the other person will instead be focused on how uninterested you are, worried that they're boring you.

Smile and make positive gestures often. Sometimes, we have moments where we might fade out, lose focus, or forget what someone said during a conversation. This is normal, and while you should be doing your best to make sure that you keep focus, a smile and a head nod is an encouraging mannerism that lets the other person know they still have your attention.

Face them and make eye contact often. You don't want

to stare directly at them, as this could cause an awkward feeling and make them feel as though there's too much pressure to talk. Maintain a normal level of eye contact and do your best to not think too much about your "staring strategy." The more you focus on eye contact, the more you'll think too hard about how you should be looking at someone.

Make your voice tone reflect your interest in the conversation as well. Even if you feel a little tired, make sure to keep energy in your voice so as not to drain the energy from the other person as well. Always keep warmth in your voice to encourage them to keep talking rather than a tone that could be cold or dismissive.

You know already that it's important to show to others that you're interested in what they have to say, even if you're just pretending. Amongst with family members it keeps the peace. Amongst peers it means that you'll be listened to when you're talking. These were skills that I needed to master when it came to setting up my digital marketing consultancy in Singapore. Creating that atmosphere where my prospective clients felt listened to, and their needs understood, was essential to our success there.

Stay Current

Be up-to-date on what's in the news, as it helps in bigger talks. If you don't know anything about what current events someone might be talking about, it might be harder for them to find a relatable topic that the two of you can discuss. The more you know about what's happening in the world, the better you can keep up with a plethora of conversations. It goes beyond just knowing what someone's talking about as well. You should strive to have something to add to the conversation, too.

Alternatively, if you aren't sure of what someone is talking about, don't be afraid to ask them. A person you're conversing with might not feel like explaining the current situation they're discussing, but they could still offer up bits of information in order to help you at least have a sense of what they're talking about.

Don't be afraid to ask questions. It's always better to admit that you don't know what someone else is talking about rather than getting caught pretending like you know something you clearly don't.

Developing Your Own Value

You should aim to develop your own value and opinion about life, relationships, work, and other various topics. The stronger sense of self you have, the easier you'll be able to share bits of information about your personality and interests with others. People can see a big difference in those that have their own idea of what might have value versus someone that doesn't really have any solid opinions of their own.

Read books. Books will open the door to so many discussions in various conversations. Even if someone else hasn't read the same book as you, you both could find relatable key points in the discussions about a certain novel.

Travel when possible. Those who have traveled a lot have the ability to see many amazing things that others don't. If you have the financial stability to do so, aim to travel as much as possible. I can't tell you how much I learned from traveling. The things we saw and people we met in China, South East Asia and other places in the world we traveled to, taught me lessons I could never learn in books. By traveling, you can broaden your perspective on life and gain plenty of interesting experiences that will always be engaging conversation topics.

Connect with more people. There's a difference between knowing a lot of people and actually connecting with them. Focus on developing strong relationships with different individuals rather than just trying to be friends with as many people as possible. Having one strong friend is more valuable than 20 friends that don't even know your last name.

Constantly challenge yourself to go out of your comfort zone. The more you can force yourself into a situation that forces learning and growth, the more you'll develop as a person, therefore developing a stronger value and overall sense of worth.

Explore Topics

Don't stay on just one topic. When you find a topic that you both relate to, it can be tempting to just talk about this all night. Use that topic to help you explore other areas of a particular person's interests. For example, if you find out that the both of you are from a small town in Idaho, you might want to just talk about that all night. Then, you both just become the people from Idaho! Instead, ask where else they might have lived, or if they do some traveling. From there, you can branch into more topics as well. Keep the level of variety as high as possible in your conversation.

Find something the other person is excited about. If you bring up a topic and notice their eyes light up or a smile spread across their face, dive deeper into that topic. Notice when someone is passionate about a certain topic so that you can expand on that and create a more interesting conversation.

Ask a series of questions about the topic to show your interest. Even if you feel like you know something about a particular area of interest, you should still ask the other person questions to see what they know and if they have anything interesting to offer. You don't want to get to a place where you just school the other person on the things that they might like or care about.

Reveal Something Personal

Sometimes, we might feel the need to keep ourselves closed off so that we don't show too much vulnerability in any given situation. You should still aim to reveal something personal about yourself, as this allows the other person to feel more connected to you.

You might want to make it seem as though you aren't flawed, but perfect people aren't relatable. Show that you're human through your flaws or a personal bit of information.

Not too personal that will make the conversation awkward. For example, if the conversation moves to a topic such as baseball, maybe you had a traumatic experience as a child that caused you to absolutely loathe the sport. Instead of diving into a topic where you talk about your childhood trauma, just tell them that you just don't feel comfortable playing that certain sport.

Maintain and Deepen Conversation

Engage the other person and share relatable information about yourself, but make sure you listen at least as much as you talk. It's easy to talk about ourselves, but no one is going to want to listen to you sit there and do all the talking for hours at a time, so give them a chance to share the same amount or more information.

Respect the other person's opinion. Don't push people to see your perspective if you find that you are arguing.

Though they might think Chicago pizza is better than New York, but you're an NYC native, don't get into a heated argument. Just agree to disagree.

Follow up the personal opinions or statement with relevant questions. Though their opinion might be different than yours, don't try to change it, just try to learn from it. Maybe they have a perspective you never even considered.

Ask more open-ended questions that dig deeper about things that matter to you. This way, instead of arguing about who's right or wrong, both of you are developing strong opinions.

What we've learned

- Show enthusiasm when talking to other people. No one is going to open up to you if you're acting like you don't care about what they have to say.
- Developing your own value is important in creating your own sense of self, which will also make small talk, and talking in general, much easier.

- Talk about things the other person is interested in, and maybe even reveal something personal so that the two of you can develop a deeper connection.

Being anxious is the quickest way to turn a conversation sour. The next chapter will discuss how to avoid this while providing important ideas to achieve a high level of confidence.

7. HOW TO STOP BEING ANXIOUS

> 66 *Worry is a thin stream of fear trickling through the mind. If encouraged, it cuts a channel into which all other thoughts are drained.*
>
> — Arthur Somers Roche

Anxiety is a powerful emotion that can greatly affect how we react in certain situations. Some people only feel anxious when they have a big event coming up, while other people struggle to leave their homes due to crippling social anxiety.

The important thing to remember about anxiety is that it won't necessarily ever go away. Anxious thoughts will always travel through our heads, but we don't always have to give them the same amount of energy. Sometimes, you just have to let the feeling of anxiety run its course but remember that how you react to that anxiety is the most important part.

We've all been in a situation where we were anxious. Maybe it was sitting for an exam. Maybe it was attending a job interview. Maybe it was when you were on a date and you really wanted to impress the other person. Anxiety is something that has plagued me all my life, starting with the aftermath of my dad moving out of our family home. Luckily, there are ways to overcome it.

The best way to overcome anxiety is to practice mindfulness. Anxiety is fear over the future or remorse for the past. The different levels of anxiety are always varying among different people, but you should still be sure that you practice the same anxiety preventative techniques that psychiatrists recommend.

Mindfulness involves making yourself grounded and present in any given moment. If you focus on your surroundings instead of your inner thoughts, you can be more connected in the moment, leading to a better memory of the situation and more involvement with those around you.

Remember that everything takes practice, and this includes reducing your anxiety. You're not going to be able to go out right this instant and not be anxious in all your conversations, but you can at least start to recognize anxious patterns and determine the best course of action to combat these certain fears.

Maintain Posture

Confident body language does more than making you look good; it makes you more memorable. A person will notice if you're confident, and they'll associate that kind of trait with you more than if you keep yourself small and closed off, not being open at all with the other person.

Stand straight and avoid slouching when sitting, and let your arms hang naturally. The more aware of your body you become, sometimes it's harder to hold it normally, but always remember to make sure you have a body language that's inviting, not one that makes you seem unimportant or forgettable.

Develop a Sense of Confidence

Do not let the fear of looking like foolish keep you away from speaking up and asking questions, or telling your own stories, and sharing your own opinions. It's much better to say something that you don't feel confident about than to not say anything at all.

Stand and sit up straight and maintain eye contact both while listening and speaking. If you give off the idea that you're overly conscious of what you're saying and that you don't wish to share any of your own opinions, it's letting the other person know that they shouldn't hold any value in you either. If you can't love yourself, or see your own worth and value, how do you expect anyone else to see it?

Be Calm and Collected

Stay calm and composed all the time to handle conversations effectively. Even if you're freaking out on the inside, worried what to say next or trying to figure out what the other person might be saying, remember to keep your cool. The other person can notice if you're feeling especially nervous, and that's what can really turn a conversation sour.

If you notice you're getting nervous, focus on your breathing and listen to what they say. Practice mindfulness during conversations by watching the way someone moves their mouth, uses their hands, and what the look in their eyes might be representing. Don't focus on yourself, but instead, turn your attention to the other person. Even if you can't keep up with *what* they're saying, you can put an emphasis on *how* they're saying it.

Laugh Appropriately

Make sure the humor you use is relevant to the situation. You might think of a funny joke or remark, but before speaking, make sure that you're not going to say anything inappropriate. Ask yourself how someone could find offense in a joke before saying anything.

Laughing when you should show that you are confident and not nervous. Make sure you're not overdoing it, however, or else others might start to wonder if you're being genuine. Laugh when others do to make sure you're not sticking out too much as someone that just laughs because they feel uncomfortable.

Don't Be in a Hurry to Talk

Allow them to talk the most while you're egging them on. When you actually think of an idea or something to share, you might start to get the feeling that you just want to spill out all your emotions and feelings. Refrain from this and instead try to make sure the other person is getting their turn in any given conversation.

Avoid Fidgeting

Fidgeting is a sign of nervousness. While you might think others don't notice what you're doing with your hands, they can at least self-consciously pick up on your different fidgets. This might lead to them being nervous as well, or they'll just wonder if you're actually paying attention to anything that they're saying.

If you feel a need to play with an item or your hands, fold your hands instead. When you feel the need to shake your leg or sway from side to side, try going for a small walk, stepping outside for some fresh air, or changing positions. If your fidgeting feels uncontrollable and changing locations isn't an option, excuse yourself to the bathroom so you can take a few minutes to calm down alone. Practice some breathing exercises so you can use different methods to calm yourself down in times of high anxiety.

Keep Your Phone Away

Using your phone while talking to someone shows lack of confidence. It can be very tempting to just pull your phone out and start looking through social media when you're feeling uncomfortable. Don't do this in front of other people, as they'll either get the idea that you're self-conscious or that you don't care about what they have to say.

Using your cell phone is a distraction and can cause a loss of interest. Even if the other person has their phone out, you might still see something online that pulls your attention away, killing all the connections you've built up by simply showing momentary disinterest in the other person. Wait until someone is finished speaking or if you're in the restroom to check your phone. If you do check your phone in front of the other person, maybe share something you saw to keep the conversation going. No one is going to want to watch a video of something random off your phone, but you could check different news stories or updates, or even some photos you've taken and share this with the person you're talking to.

What we've learned

- Anxiety is a feeling we all have at different levels, but you must make sure that you don't let this rule your life.
- Stay confident even when you might not be feeling your best. You want to remain calm and collected and keep a steady pace with your talking, so others don't pick up on your lack of confidence.
- Don't fidget or play on your phone in order to make sure that you're staying fully connected to any given conversation.

Being calm and confident is crucial in any social settings. But some of you might have another question: how do I deal with the people I don't like?

Well, as Melanie Moushigian Koulouris once said, "Everyone has a story to tell, a lesson to teach, and wisdom to share..." we should try our best to get to know someone before we start to judge that person. In the next chapter, we will discuss the importance of not casting too much judgment on those around you.

8. DON'T MISJUDGE ANYONE

> 66 *If I stop judging other people, I free myself from being judged, and I can dance!*
>
> — Patti Digh

Unfortunately, many of us have fallen into a situation in which judging another person is easier than finding the good in them. We have all the tools it takes to pick someone else's actions apart, but when it comes to seeing the good in them, that can be a challenge.

Especially when it comes to ourselves. After the failure of three different consecutive business projects I began ripping all my actions and decisions apart, but it was Linda, my life coach, who helped me to understand that there was more to their failure than what I was seeing. She, and Michelle, helped me to see the good in myself and that taught me to also see the good in others.

Know that the more you judge someone else, the more you're judging yourself. Your brain is trained to have certain thoughts, so if you put an emphasis on how someone looks or acts, it's a reflection on how you see your own looks and actions. For example, if you're constantly judging the shoes someone else wears, making assumptions on a person just because they're not wearing certain types of shoes, you probably put a lot of emphasis on your own shoes. Judging yourself too harshly can cause serious anxiety, so if you start going easier on others, you'll likely go much easier on yourself, too.

Don't Make Assumptions

Avoid making quick judgments about other people. Remember that the first thought you have isn't always the true view that you have. For example, a person might be wearing a dirty shirt that looks like it hasn't been washed. Your first thought might be, "Why couldn't they wear a nicer shirt?" But instead of coming to this conclusion, try to think of all the reasons they couldn't wear something nicer. Maybe they can't afford nice clothes and have to shop second hand. Perhaps their washer or dryer is broken, or maybe their house burned down, and they lost all their clothes. You never know what someone is going through, so you can't make assumptions until you know all the facts.

Be Open-Minded

Come out of your comfort zone. Though it's important to have strong morals and beliefs, you can't let these become strict rules for how you see the world. You should always be altering the way you think towards a more inviting path of growth and in a way that invites positivity and continual learning.

Be more welcoming to new ideas. Don't shut someone out of your life just because they seem like they might have a different perspective. You could end up learning something very valuable from them that you wouldn't know if you cut them out of your life.

Avoid criticizing them when they tell you anything

personal. You might want to come back with a, "What are you talking about?" when they share that they don't like something you do. Instead, tell them something like, "That's an interesting perspective," making sure to not break them down for their thoughts and opinions. More often than not, they might not be that strong in their beliefs, and you could have some influence on that person if you stay positive instead of trying to "win" the conversation.

Look for the Good

Look for the good in people. Not the other way around. Our society has conditioned us to look for people's flaws, mostly because of the capitalist ideologies created by different advertisers. Practice looking for the good in the person, because even someone that you see as the world's mortal enemy might carry an important idea that could change the way you think.

Ask yourself questions about the good thing you can find in this person. Everyone has at least one good thing about them that makes them an individual.

. . .

What we've learned

- The harsher we judge other people, the harsher we judge ourselves.
- You can't assume anything about anyone, no matter what certain signs or signals they're giving off.
- The more open-minded you are, the easier it will be to keep a neutral perspective.

In the next chapter, we'll discover how to end a conversation in the right way to ensure that from beginning to end, you have a meaningful connection.

9. ENDING A CONVERSATION GRACEFULLY

> *People will forget what you said, people will forget what you did, but people will never forget how you made them feel.*
>
> — MAYA ANGELOU

It's important to remember that after you've finished speaking with someone, they're not likely going to remember everything that you said. They're going to remember certain ideas, but they don't have a script of all the different things that you specifically reiterated. Instead, they're going to remember if you were polite, funny, and generous, or if you were rude, cocky, and arrogant. It's important to not let yourself get hung up on every individual thing that was said and instead aim to make sure that you've managed to create a positive experience for the other person.

Say Thank You and Goodbye

Remember the guy with the baby advice whom I mentioned earlier? I was in the elevator with him and I asked about his children to make up a conversation that wasn't related to my pitch for investment. He ended up chatting with me and giving me baby-related advice all the way to my car. Eventually he wound up investing in a line of gym equipment I had designed. It was this incident that taught me the importance of leaving the conversation on a high. Because we'd had a good chat about his children he remembered me later on and already had a positive attitude towards me.

Ending the conversation can be very challenging, as you might not always know what to say. Always remember to say thank you to the person that you've been conversing with. If the conversation seems to be dying or the other person is losing interest, say something like, "Well thank you for giving me the time to talk today." This is also a great signal that the conversation might be over and it's time to move on.

Life would be so much easier if we could just walk away when we want to without having to go through all those goodbyes. There are plenty of people who will say, "I hate goodbyes," but seriously, who likes them? Goodbyes can be sad, awkward, and uncomfortable. In order to alleviate this tension, remind the person of how much you enjoyed their conversation. You can try thanking them with phrases like:

- It's been so great talking to you, I've really learned a lot.
- I appreciate that we were able to get together and have this conversation.
- I've enjoyed discussing different things with you and think you have a really great perspective on (specific topic).

End with a Handshake

Shaking someone's hand at the end of the conversation is a great way to give the person one last chance to remember you. It's a physical reminder of the time that you shared together and a great way to leave a lasting impression on them.

Always make sure that your hand is "shakable." Don't shake someone's hand when yours is covered in grease, food, or sweat. If you just ate a large meal and you know the night's coming to an end, go to the restroom to wash your hands just to make sure you're not going to leave them with the lasting impression that you have bad hygiene.

Your grip is important as well. Having a firm handshake is important, but you also don't want to be remembered as the person that almost broke their fingers. Always consider the other person's culture as well. If you're not sure what's appropriate, keep your hands available and lead them out the door with your arm so they know that if they wanted to shake your hand, they could. Some cultures don't find it acceptable for a man to shake a woman's hand, or for people to touch at all. If you're doing some international traveling, be sure to investigate what the proper handshaking moments are.

Referencing the Next Conversation

When ending a conversation, it's important to make sure that you're setting up the relationship for future opportunities. This might include simple phrases like, "I look forward to seeing you again," or it could be something more complex like, "We're still on for drinks on Thursday at 5:30, right?" You want to make sure your relationship is open for the next time that you can get together.

Even if you think it's the last time you'll ever see a person in your life, at least let them know that you hope to see them again by saying something like, "I hope to see you soon," or, "Let's keep in touch, so we can get together again."

Asking Questions

Sometimes, you might want to ask some questions when ending certain conversations. Maybe this will include asking them if they had a nice evening, enjoyed their meal, or if they need anything else before departing. Make sure that you're taking care of their needs even in the final moments that the two of you are together.

This shows that even though you're done with the conversation, you still greatly care about the other person and their needs. They'll be more likely to remember you if you give a clear effort in maintaining your relationships.

What we've learned

- Ending conversations are hard, but you should be prepared to make sure it ends gracefully.
- Practice handshaking to make sure that this moment of physical touch will help you leave a lasting impression.
- Always thank the other person for talking to you and remind them of when you might be able to have a discussion again in the future.

AFTERWORD

I appreciate your decision when choosing to read this book. I hope that you have learned some valuable information throughout this reading. Don't be afraid to reread any information you might have missed and take notes to make sure you're pulling the relevant and applicable information out, so you can reference it quicker if you must.

If you worry about starting conversations, write down some of the conversation topics or other questions to ask in order to have them handy when you're talking with other people. You might feel foolish having this tool with you, but there's no shame in being prepared for any conversation that might pop up.

Remember that the key to improvement still lies within

yourself. As much as I would love to be in your ear during important conversations, I can't. You have to remember these techniques in order to use them when going throughout various social interactions.

I encourage you to practice what you have learned through the book. Remember that the key to talking to anyone is practice. Just like everything else in life. You aren't always going to win. Sometimes, you might have a conversation with someone and you go home, only regretting the things that you said or wishing you had even said more.

Once a conversation has ended, there isn't anything to do. If you do have regrets over certain aspects of a conversation, just look at it as a learning experience and not something to beat yourself up over. You'll get better at talking with each and every conversation you have. The most important thing to remember is that practice makes perfect!

I am always happy to give others the benefit of my experiences and knowledge, but I am also still learning as I go along. We are never done growing and developing as people, and this is an important thing to remember. So don't get down on yourself for turning to a book like this, a self-help book. Instead of feeling down, you should feel empowered because you are taking control of your life, identifying a weakness and trying to improve yourself. There is absolutely nothing wrong with that as that is the way I came to ditch my desk job, take up a whole new direction to end up with the job of my dreams and the family of my dreams. With the right tools and exercises, you can achieve your dreams too.

AUTHOR'S NOTE

Thank you so much for taking the time to read my book. I hope you have enjoyed reading this book as much as I've enjoyed writing it. If you enjoyed this book, please consider leaving a review on Amazon. Your support really means a lot and keeps me going.

ABOUT THE AUTHOR

Steven Hopkins is a personal trainer, entrepreneur, life coach, and author on a mission to awaken people to their innate talents and purpose so they can leave their mark in the world.

Steven holds a Master's degree in Behavioral Science and specializes in the areas of success, motivation, self-discipline, communication, NLP techniques, psychology, and human behavior.

When he isn't helping his clients attain their maximum potential, Steven Hopkins enjoys meditating, playing extreme sports, and traveling across the globe. He also loves spending quality time with his lovely wife and his two beautiful children.

Made in the USA
Coppell, TX
05 September 2020